CONGOTRONIC

KUHL HOUSE POETS

edited by Mark Levine and Emily Wilson

CONGOTRONIC

POEMS BY SHANE BOOK

University of Iowa Press, Iowa City

University of Iowa Press, Iowa City 52242
Copyright © 2014 by Shane Book
www.uiowapress.org
Printed in the United States of America

Design by Ashley Muehlbauer

The University of Iowa Press is a member of
Green Press Initiative and is committed to
preserving natural resources.

Printed on acid-free paper

ISBN: 978-1-60938-307-7 (pbk)
ISBN: 978-1-60938-308-4 (ebk)
LCCN: 2014935646

Our music is a secret order.

LOUIS ARMSTRONG

CONTENTS

ACKNOWLEDGMENTS

Grateful acknowledgment is made to the editors of the magazines in which these poems first appeared: *1913*, *American Letters and Commentary*, *Boston Review*, *Dandelion*, *Denver Quarterly*, *Fence*, *Harp & Altar*, *Hyperallergic*, *Jubilat*, *Lana Turner*, *Obsidian*, *Omniverse*, *Qwerty*, *Rattapallax*, *The Rumpus*, *Saint Mary's Magazine*, and *VOLT*.

Acknowledgment is made as well to the following anthologies: *A Face to Meet the Faces: An Anthology of Contemporary Persona Poetry* (eds. Stacey Lynn Brown and Oliver de la Paz, University of Akron Press); *From the Fishouse* (eds. Matt O'Donnell and Camille T. Dungy, fishousepoems.org); *Gathering Ground: A Reader Celebrating Cave Canem's First Decade* (eds. Toi Derricotte, Cornelius Eady, and Camille T. Dungy, University of Michigan Press); *The Great Black North: Contemporary African Canadian Poetry* (eds. Valerie Mason-John and Kevan Anthony Cameron, Frontenac House); *The Harp & Altar Anthology* (eds. Keith Newton and Eugene Lim, Ellipsis Press); *Poetry Mountain* (ed. John Struloeff, poetrymountain.com); *Revival: An Anthology of Black Canadian Writing* (ed. Donna Bailey Nurse, McClelland & Stewart); and *The Rumpus Original Poetry Anthology* (ed. Brian Spears, therumpus.net).

The Flagelliforms were published as a chapbook by speCt! books.

This work was made possible by the support of the Canada Council for the Arts, the Cave Canem Foundation, the Chalmers Arts Fellowship, the Ford Foundation, the Jerome Foundation, the MacDowell Colony, the Naropa University Summer Writing Program, the Ontario Arts Council, Randolph College, Instituto Sacatar Brazil, Stanford University, the University of Iowa, and the Wallace Stegner Fellowship.

My thanks, also, to Tim Black, Archie Book, Kimberley Book, Lorna Book, Forrest Gander, Adrian Harewood, Brenda Hillman, T. Geronimo Johnson, David Lau, Mark Levine, Damian Rogers, Ilya Simakov, Cole Swensen, and Emily Wilson.

CONGOTRONIC

AFRICAN EVENING

I had a thing for mange.
Her skin was fluorescent with it.
The open canoe made smooth, curling sounds.
It smelled like the man I am told is mother.
Mother sped his brain on pills.
He limped.
He gripped mother's leg and begged.
The long open canoe had a wind inside
and a yellow sky and a smell of mother.
I went to the docks to pray.
The trees were yellow, the trees were orange
and her panties had been cut away.
I had a thing for docks and praying on the little bronze pipes.
I stained them with my fluid.
I had a bald thing, a bashed in thing, a thing for her grease.
In my arms I held an end of the long canoe and slit it
sternum-first into the sea.

WORLD TOWN

Entirely windless, today's sea; of these waters' many names
the best seemed "field-of-pearl-leaves," for it smelled like
    the air
in the house he built entirely of doors: pink school door,
gold of the burnt hotel, two old church blues, the abandoned
bank's steel doors singular and immovably wedged over
the family's heads though as with everything corroding
the sense of themselves slipping away in the heat,
falling through the day's brightness the way soldiers
once fell upon him walking home with a bucket of natural
water as he had been recalling the town square
before the tannery's closing: he and his father shopping
on horseback in the noon *Praça* where they first saw
a man crouched under a black shroud, what his father called
a camera. His father forgot the incident immediately, but
for years the man asked whomever if they remembered
a camera, vegetable stalls, the butcher holding the cleaver,
a horseshoeing shop, purple berries, the long cassava valley
    haze,
fishnets, a few crab baskets and browning nets
drying by the ice cream shop, seven taverns,
a small, unused ferry terminal, a map on its wall outlining
the island in blue, the names Good Dispatch, Lover's Bridge
pointed to by a mermaid of skin whiter than anyone
on this island of Angola's descendants, her red hair.

SECURITY OF THE FIRST WORLD

This place I have not been.
But alone. Other
possibilities perhaps
and even if I am
of two sliding partitions:
the trees' spacing, tidal
flats punctured by tubular
posts, children—I cannot
arrive at such days,

a fly bumping glass.
Faces may take me
to a station to pick out
hands from stacks of hands.
I continue meaning work
on the metal up into
palatial sound, bricking
a total music of the past.

Water, yes. Include
the hacking text as an excellent
first step, and a flying
picture slashing in ether
flashing a short-lived
shadow. In fact she worked
every day, wedged
between moments of thinking

new cities and a glass bird
furred in monosyllables
no one had bothered
to adopt. She did not
die. A truck came
collecting things and climbing
into the back she entered
a crushingly red sea.

LAST

The difficulty of staying
on after all the sandstone has been looted
off the sand-sea barges. There's a place you don't wanna
be. Where the wind eats the evening's seed
and the pummeled trees grow to look like tonsils.

One or two cries rang out just before you arrived.
A wandering drumming washed in:
your tar lady.
I've been worried about these ropy clouds
and her. She's a problem, whipping post or no.

Strap on your feet.
They fit well. They're the color of dirt.
If you want to leave
you won't take the skins.
Skins are useful.

Anyway you are staying here.
That's what the chain
of insects is for.

PORE TUNE

Talls up our helmeted stingers.
Marches through the torn up zero farm,
casing. Dew boss: ants in tow.
A cup of paintings, atonal moves,
a row of mounts, the ordnance for delousing
colors, the noosing glass. Two bosses
by the forgone blank. It is now or.
Ear turnovers shall ever maroon us.
With our stash of latitudinal rope,
heavy kneels on a guard else he bark out,
"Line and door," else he squeal out, "Fast root
gondola is here." Lay shears, grab and ran,
only fool me can fool me. Through me beat
an orbit a secure deck whereupon
eggs bring Negresses in dugouts.
Carnal diamond lids lidding the loose
dusk sea. Do it on tight.
A knot called Sudan Throat.

JANELAS

I have a home in my son's hand.
The pier is out, the quay closed at noon.
You can sob, so be it, as if dates, as
though you had an oven of dough
everyone wanted. Day, I'm a over it;
out rowing an O.K. used pear,
sailing your barcode, you shop with the pain
you're out now, avowing.
Our row cake vice squeezing through
sewer hour, I sail mystery O
sewer! Made on that pall of rat veil
A forms a dream navy
in the unclear I don't miss saying.

MACK DADDY MANIFESTO

*"Ultimately, when stubborn historical facts had dispersed all
intoxicating effects of self-deception, this form of Socialism
ended in a miserable fit of the blues."*
—KARL MARX & FRIEDRICH ENGELS

A spectre is haunting Europe
but I feel the sun cocooning
in a triple-breasted track suit

> when I think of you. Thus we
> obtain our concept of the unconscious
> from the theory of repression, a sweet finish

after the bitter pills of floggings and bullets,
my Tender-roni, my Maytag Blue—
for real, you like them dresses? I'll bag the whole rack—let
the ruling classes tremble

"But you Communists would introduce
community of women!" screams
the chorus.

> All I'm thinkin' is Sugar,
> African me till you African't
> leave every jaw
>
> dropped, cocked and locked,
> freeze the whole

　　　　　　　　　　homeboy corner crew:
　　　　　　　　　　Pope – Czar,
　　　　　　　　　　Metternich – Guizot,
　　　　　　　　　　French Radicals – German police spies

all sewing duodecimo editions
of New Jerusalem, this special organ appearing
to be the muscular apparatus of
old Europe's powers
in holy alliance to exorcise

this special organ appearing to need
　　　　　　　　　　my help. I do what I can. "Hola hotty!" I
　　　　　　　　　　　holla –
　　　　　　　　　　when what I really mean is,
　　　　　　　　　　　"Baby got back!" as here
　　　　　　　　　　and there among the spindly trees the
　　　　　　　　　　　contest
　　　　　　　　　　breaks out into riots: What does it mean
　　　　　　　　　　　when we say

making something conscious? Have not
the Christians already declaimed:

Underneath this thug armor: a corn ear of nuclear cornea
　　　fission.
It fuels my new clear cornrow vision.

All fixed frozen relations,
their ancient
and venerable trains
swept away,
all new-forms
antiquated before
they can ossify? 　　　　　Sho'nuff,

at fifty feet your party smile puts a wrinkle
in a salt fish patty substitute for longing for the father,
the germ religions spawned. By days, by degrees they
sink into their fanatical, superstitious belief
in the miraculous effects of their social science.
And you thought I was a player
'cause you heard some other guy lace that last line
to your little sister? Little did you know he wasn't nothing
but a biter, player-hating 'cause the ladies
love me despite the fact my hair is nappy—

    the annexation taking place as when
     a foreign language is appropriated,
     namely, by translation—

unlike
"True" Socialism, which appears to kill
with one stone,
spreads like an epidemic,
and is fore-most a body-ego.
Of course this is only hypothesis,
there's no museum space
to offer – exhibit A:
    the ever-mean talk show hosts,
    bitter preachers, dirty rappers,
    all up in my shit,
    running their mouths
    like they was me,

    but winding up lipping blisters:

     Whereas the Communists have no need
      to introduce
     free love; it has existed almost from time

immemorial, and on and on to the break
of dawn, to let us now
take wage labor:

clinical observation showing
circumstances where hate changes to love,
love to hate and

our bourgeoisie taking great
pleasure in seducing each other's wives.
Real real soon,
as in yester-after-noon, I need to step to
your crib, and tell you how I feel the proletarians
have nothing to lose but their world to win.

Be ready chula,
I'm a move the mood up.
You gonna call me "Vision master,"

Ergo, those who work, acquire nothing and those who
acquire anything, do not work!

Ain't it all good,
ain't it morning before you know it,
ain't my suits crazy insulated
with gold leaf history

in which free
development of each
is the condition
for free development of all.

Likewise it has to feed a man,
instead of being fed to him. He
becomes an appendage of the machine,

but it is only simple yak fur
lining my boots
that I need if I got you . . .
                    I'll make
                    all that is solid melt into air
                    all that is holy profaned

THE COLLECTED NOVELLAS
OF GILBERT RYLE

THEY ARE NOT BITS OF CLOCKWORK

Node where may none die poor,
false, yellow. Node from whence
my nesting eye pours. Last creature,
as of daylight snorting swallowing
a lunar rail. It drills in. Bright
craving, all incredible. O banjo.
O quiet lantern. A protest
of lost astronauts stroking
through a thick strobe.
Nodding eye, Nodding eye.
Node where may none die.

THEY ARE AS ROBINSON
CRUSOES, COMMANDING

Sick on a quay. Quay-sick. There was sickness
on the quay. On the little cement area, a mass
laying on of hands. Over the spacious abacus
he sung out nine untested terrors. Hay strands
tied on. A pair of parakeets bolted
to a wave. From a blue mug, a hat trick
of notes left sticking straight out of the meniscus
of the cooling Paraguayan tea.

Node where may none die poor, almond,
mundane, but in this very *Yes* keep the body
at a distance. One Satan-boat cuss after
another, in swaths unamaranthine runs
the body deep in as a resent is. Pseudo-lore,
lead dollar, sin desk and sword o' smoke
so the body all tapered. The body would
lead well, if he on tender gears, spectral
switches, were to lay ever a sober bray.
A bad day for a grim taker, a serious gas.
Iced-in, the tabernacle.

THEY CANNOT BE TAKEN TO BITS

His manhandle was ever "Bat and Toe."
This freedom, he thought, is what makes
his subliminal feel relationship to it
profound, a farther land ever-shimmering.
From somewhere nearby, core odor
of day lily. He set off in pursuit. He kept
a trio of daggers under his dirndl
for just such emergencies.

THEY ARE INTRINSICALLY
PHOSPHORESCENT

Hoses keyed into a defoliated brier refuge.
Roasted meat scent off in the offing.
Stilled in play, in newest row of diggings
round the burnt greenish limestone manor,
one *folie à deux*. An oblique leaf
on the breeze changing course by less
than ninety degrees. A Marine chopper
posing a hole as day blazes below. Some
could fall in a dialed-in instant.
Alert, alert, then gone out into the length
we who you are.

THEY ARE NOT MOTIONS, SUITES, CABINS

I was drawing fewer iguanas, bees,
asps. I was sticking to a murder,
a last hunger. Nothing swinging.
"He, I." and then "Don't." with a shard
of coral, wrote her, on the lens of the ski
mask in the painting titled:
"On the depth and privacy of his Yes."

THEY FOMENT A REVOLT

Unfurls a yellow bib you run down.
Horns you as furred fanged O's rain
from the unspooled ceilings, sealings
of armadillo pelt and brush-cut fresh cane.
Walls sprayed winter hostage camouflage.
Thrown dirt floor with bare aim.
Sewn into their own resurrection lair,
the lassoed posse of eleven.
A graffitoed dis from a rune you gotta
see. You got ruins and then you got
ruins and a hard shuttered torpor
of shuttered doors. Unlace yourself,
a heady is upon us. House grease
on the barcodes, glass gates, barcodes.
Every. Only.

THEY HAVE A PRIVATE CAREER

His boots were broken. When he walked
they said, "Cold only rawed ideas."
He had been at the Colony for many years.
He had been busy culling spores
from the frothy air as the para-mechanical
cloud test come in low over the valley.
Into the late air as into a darkened,
humid dirt basement, he yelled
"Where Tos?" and, "You OKs?"
until the distance became unbearable.

THEY ARE OF AN EXTRAORDINARY
FERAL TERRITORY

Livid A. Alert A. Low A.
Skated-over garden, don't A be.
A, welled as soda pop. Glass zero A.
Culling A, lulled by mulchy aches
powered by the brass memorial
of one bile-ish babe in the arms
of invention. Invention there to point
out, where to get, what to call. O, A.
A he zap at or flay as the lowest
all-moor down there. He wanna see
air, pace of one spare dawn that spare.
A, lasso latent but at the ready,
setting forth into the frontier.
A in the mummification lab,
cradling the glistening leg of
one delicately peeled camel. Quietly
rocking A, repeating the low say:
Air here is a con. Unviolent to scale
of one fantastic rushing-by. Azul were A.
Rio! As you were, A. As woolen.

THEY COME HOME IN A TORRENT
OF LAUGHTER AND A NUBIAN
EUNUCH-POWERED LITTER

1

Sea algae and sea-era dust.

2

Loosed postage randomly pasted as an old tableau vivant I
    always held me over,

3

over on a wall of the old chateau—a high-test

4

contusion of refugeed bees milling round for a chance to
    beat out
beats on the taut skin

5

of my only wholly tuned conundrum. Hold me, I've been
    put on hold.

6

Low in panoramic dale or hoarse from attempting to wail,
    those I ran me from

7

was guests, centipedal nodes vastly scurrying.

8

From where may I not pour me over, a wispy helmsman
nearly undone in fevered looking? Of sea algae pairs

9

trying it out in a porous land. Of chain-excesses hand
in hand with the first ferocious no-see-ums,

10

of a season.

11

A singing bridge scuffed then scuttled by a roar of cleats be
    a wriggling troubled bowl,

12

be a bad hole.

13

With a lung-full heaped full of ballast for scope,
I come in low

14

over the false-eyed leafy copses

15

bent in for the lack or how two who love do a deal
to steal a moment in

16

from the sea of throws.

*

THE IVORIAN "BECAUSE BECAUSE"

Touch grasper to a hotted thing I am split largish nubby digit I am loping basketball thwacks bulbous charcoal-shaded head I am monster Sharpy marker squeaks spelled smell on paper I am three chiggers burrow dermis leaving three trace itch-holes I am thrice over a monumental runny wind jolt from touching I am inflamed flying insect space heater timbre I am swung-jumped excitement after the first bite I am after after I am because because I am a burst of was I am gunshot boom and echo jumped into and into I am fortune cake palm wrapper crackle I am jangling street geometry randomness I am fenestrations from the first incisions I am smoldering pig shit bouquet in the somewhat sun I am initial molecular post-swig surge of the sugared I am fingered winter metal joy I am from an Exact-o-edge premier incursion comes an exacted feeling [maybe] I am eyes switched out by the foot of the dark spiral stairs

A LABORIOUS WAKEFULNESS OR WAS IT A MOST UNAPOLOGETIC WHISTLING IN THE EAR

I lack full, clear proof of his skin a drum.
Have I always been under-sided, a quandary's
viscous lowered aura, *for example there is the fact*
I'm inclined to disbelieve *the violent vapours*
of black bile, a stab, a treason mounted. Am I
really seeking to assure the delegates assembled
in the cerebella what lies beyond the shadow
of the doubled shout. On Radio However—
whose throat I hesitate to sit by the fire attired
in a brocaded dressing gown: day, un-arisen day.
About which writhing dream do I curl. Pretend
you're on Zeus, on Coltrane—yes, they are aural
truths and no, I do hesitate to hear the rusting killer
roses arriving. A key in, is a big reverse decay horse.
A killer is: spattered your life a dirt viola. Is there
a core ambiguity to the small un-armoured hand
bobbing near the beach. Your pen say, "On na floor
is da pride era. On li'l roommate day whom can we
know?" What proves the head is not of a resilient
earthenware. Even me, in-country, on panting,
I'm unsure who or what delimits the third shift from
to sky to sky to sky. I'm inclined to disbelieve
the three-phased gesture of "complete" reading. Yo,
send a bad onion, lacking glory, a day-glow hum and O
am I truly in a Potawatomi state of mind. Do I believe

in the will as hinge or tinged trilling. I am in doubt about, "So be it, traveler," undecided as to whether pumpkin could be the initial building block. Quantities sell. *For example there is the fact that I am here*.

THE COLONY MATING SONG

Keep a me. On your furlough ladle sin
into your bow. Keep a vacancy, a buoy a bear
out there you've got. Eaves are cared for,
a vacancy, all of it to do. Elk tracks,
a kayak serene. No, go on. Do have blown
on you, by that me-Elk. A paired down,
a dowel straight out and on fire says:
to go on doing dong audio, says to all Elks
wearing pasties on a pour down day.
No is toy. Elk a dared head on glinting pike
now go on do yo' thang where a crude total,
do where men, a bath hole, a length of re-bar,
alert as a little team moan: a little ye, a little
tooth. L-shaped mirror and door crack a good
jar. Does any of you? Day 1: lost cue responder.
Day 2: consent you have a each. Day 3: Others.
Day 3: You, hoarse, on low in an infinite.
Give me your hand, O glossed-to-sorrows.
A beast toes the lash. All

masts.

BRONZE AGE

Their revolution painted on a wall. Revolution
scent in the rust-colored dirt, and the rat-heavy
palms, and the blue diesel smaze over the former
capital. We waited. On the corner, insistent laughter.
On the corner, a turned over bus—flame bathed

to the metal. Our tape measures cocked,
as per our orders. We were given
a belt each and a night. Mine was short-haired,
with jagged white gear teeth and a dirt-sniffing
mechanism for quicker dirt sifting

and much data to desist. Lots: "Encada barrio . . ."
and "our ideas are our weapons." Among other things.
Revolution, revolution. Faint image of the revolution's
big man on the plaza clock. Drawn in wrought iron.
Splashed on a smock. The sounds we watched for:

night wind cracking canvas sails; wood stick
rhythmically striking wood stick; hastily made
motorcades' ragged sirens. The revolution?
Through our high powered geigers: twin-stroke
underbuzz of revolution's engine; the puttering

three-wheeled revolution; the landless campesinos
beaten by pots and pans into land and nothing
we could do. They resented our husks.
"Of two eyes one always lies," this we knew. We planned
removing the other, replacing it with Jefferson dirt:

dirt of the sea, empire dirt, wind down from the north
dirt, father dirt, dirt of scallions and ghost
galleons. The elephant god Jefferson. Trident
in one hand, another with axe, snake in another
and in another his reigns, steering his eight-rat team,

as through the green clouds they steam.
On Jefferson's neck a lush green alligator hung
from a bone chain like a hymn. As always. Family
bones, yet distant; somewhat empirical and fencing
the hill, long shards of oxidized metal. There went

tradition, bronze titan. The balcony scene:
swarms of wetblack hair surrounding
wetblack rocks on the tree-less frozen
sand expanse. Once the show trials were over
we would get to work, but quietly. Such were our orders.

Swimming style analysis, certain constellations
notated from the tattered revolutionary cupolas'
ceilings, hands to secure a detainee's head (placement
and number). In their revolutionary stories the sound
of dirt on animal skin drums was like the sound

of a blinking eye roving wild in its socket was like . . .
Their revolution had its big man and its new man tales
of the monolith sky. We had our love.

CHINESE BLOW UP DOLL

It was only in his mind.

Ain't no thing with the power

Of sun   heat   creation   screaming

River   voodoo   juju

Beautiful   first   day   of Ramadan

Sunset over   Ramallah.

In 1960 I was a Negro.

Over 100 Negro
Pounds melted
his mind.

Ain't no new thing.

Washed out baggy faced whores ain't
No new thing.

He was moving

but it was only in his mind.

Lunchmeat on the first day
of Ramadan.
West Side, West Side, bro.
Westbank, bra.
Mos def
your friend is CIA.

FREETOWN

The ear sometimes says "I am in love."

Waiting on the fortieth floor before the sunlit window in
the tilt.

The ear gets you an elevator.

It does not sit on the door, drinking juice, winter theory.

"We bombed the place, but not the people."

It says it is a silver cube.

A secret is no one around.

It tracks the numbers.

No emergencies would not benefit from keeping track of
the numbers?

The green door to a small room made of sleet.

And the occupations: Sniper, Pensioner, Clerk.

You have to decide: Where are the nomads?

The clink of little flames.

The smoke of burning trees we can't hear.

EVERYWHERE

Cheeks marked with the white inedible scales
I tried to resist, swallowing the chalky paste
until it blooded me. Militant payola of loose
aluminum rubbed each night. Meanwhile
I'm not in school.

Head down, bumps
on my linings, wrists, I walked
to the square 17th de Septembre.
They told me a meeting will finish it.
My name written on paper notes shoved under candles
and the red curtains flying in neighbors' windows
and the mammal hair threading the loaves
and someone wanting the huts in my eyes
[burnt to the ground.]

I prayed on the bronze pioneer. I played
a string attached to a stick.

Tall, clicking tree
mildly shading
my dangling feet.

 I waited in my mouth.

H . N . I . C .
(Head Nigger In Charge) – B-Side, Club Remix

"Bow wow wow yip-pee yo yip-pee yey, where
my dogs at, bark wit me now . . ."
— LIL' BOW WOW

Bow to the one in the white suit, the Stick Up King
of Jersey City—I got lucky—Miss Ella was a little
girl when I was borned, and she claimed me. It was
like that and this was like this. It was like wow
to the dark-skinned shortie in the shiny dress,
she got the floss and the flo and the itchy
shimmy. This was not Normandy where there are
many cows. This was where we had prayer
meeting any time, we went to the white folks'
church and there was no whiskey on the place no, no,
honey, no whiskey, and every morning round the way
we'd say Wow to the crushed can collector,
yeah, that funked-out guy we down wit—
he one street off from cool and your moms
now, but someone say coming up he'd buck her
down on a barrel and beat the blood out of her—
someone say he was this close to making Bronx
Science. They should know. My owners, my white
people, my old mistress, wrote me a letter telling
me how terrible it was at a dance one night
when a tall, gauchy American mashed my toe. They

say I made a sound that sounded like Yip, I think
his name is P, and I think his Q is—who axed
to join the white boy alliance anyway? I mean I never
seed my father in my life but you could always see
the little negro children marching on the levee
on their way to school, blue Appleton Spelling Books
up in front of their faces, chanting: *Both bit the nigger,
and they was both bad!* Much later, they would paint
YO, YOU SMELL LIKE ASS, YO! on the flag
of the High School for Humanities until one mornin'
the dogs begun to bark, and in minutes the plantation
was covered in Yankees. They were polite, told us:
Non, je n'etais pas jolie. Mais j'avais un teint de roses,
and put food in a trough and even the littlest niggers
gathered round and et. Foremost of these *protégés*
of Mother was the old mulatto, Célestine. "Yip" was not
her name but she answered to it when we was little G's,
running through the bodega with the buffet that smelled
like pee. Back then my only concern was getting my
leather satchel where I hid Mother's diamonds. That was
what I wanted, that was where I went. *Yey* is what
you wanted, *that* was where you went. And if you
like us, you hit the curtain booth back by the Panama
bananas where the doctors held a consultation,
where the suckers for corn rows and manicured
toes hung their shined out arms, exclaiming,
"*Oui mon ami*, you have made a mistake,
my army don't imitate doorway ass-whuppin
systems!" He said she meant that she would sell
him, then put the money in her pocket. She said
he meant I knows how to raise flax dogs who wonder
where you at, and ladies where you at, all the ballin-ass

niggas in the candy cars, all the girls in the house
that can buy the bar, lemme hear you say he
was on the staff of "Andrew's American Queen,"
a New York magazine, and he deluged me with poetry, so.
So, George, little more than a boy, was allowed
to take charge. He shouted: At some point you gonna see
my slouch as I slow thug toward you in my crispy
clothes! The family bitterly opposed his going into law,
a southern gentleman had to be a planter
for Virginia was synonymous with dancing
was synonymous with Yes'm, I been here a right smart
while, not, Bark and holla all you want, at some point
I'm gonna fake you to the bridge! I mean at the time dueling
was not very popular. Everyone knew "Wit" wasn't all
it and a bucket of chicken, you had to have game
and a platinum chain to step to this. And besides, at times,
she developed *les boutons* or pimples on her face.
Me, I got my nameplate etched in the corner lecture booth
at Cokie's, the Glock scholars taking constant
dictation. Several claimed their fathers were Sicilians
who came up the river as beggars on pack boats
selling oysters, bananas, apples. They sailed to
Paris for medical treatment. That was where *they* went.
They was a box with eleven hams in that grave.
It didn't bother me, no sir. I had been dressed in deep
mourning for over a year. *They* wanted her to be perfect—
for when a sugar planter walked the streets
of New Orleans with his cottonade britches, alpaca coat,
panama hat and gold-headed cane, he was the King of
Creation. To all he would quietly declaim, Now hear this,
it's the mad bling in my pocket, jingling, now hear me
dismiss this classic witness defense quick as a weekend

trip to Vegas, city of red-roofed portopotties, bean shake
slushies and more ice than you can graft to the fender
of my gold Escalade. But it didn't bother me none, no sir.
Most nights I fell asleep wearing earrings made from old
gutta percha buttons, tiny baskets carved from the shells
of large pecans, I didn't care. Plus, I had to check
on my snakes. The one called slavery lay with his head pointed
south, and the one called freedom lay with his head pointed
north. I knows how to grow a snake. You grow it,
and when it's grown, you pull it clean up out of the ground
till it kinda rots. And all night the children's chorus lays
the chorus down: *Both bit the nigger, and they was both bad!*
And in the cobblestone streets some Pimp King
of Something be shoutin', Now hear this, I gotta bounce now,
I gotta ounce now—watch it, this big dog is leashless—

FLAGELLIFORMS

FLAGELLIFORM 61: TILTED AWAY

1

I broke off the dangling shrub   and inserted it   above my
   ear.
Bent in at the belly   I sweated,   to fit   to try to fit.

2

The dangling shrub   was bruised.
It moved a little move   and Lady Song-of-Jamestown
said in my hear: Why   is broken.

3

Spooked   I
leapt   a leafy thwart
into my thinking vessel   the aluminum canoe
and in my here said Lady Song-of-Jamestown:
"Why   its smelters long ago felled at The-Task-Is-
   Incomplete,   a falling
artist felling them   name of
The-Coriander-of-Mother-and-Child
who wears   crown of shells   partly concealing
a turban of layered light."

4

I stared straight ahead,   paddling.

My canoe walls hung with barkcloth   a giant dentalium
and four figureheads in lignified paste   (We watching).

The ivory one called,   Tapping-Out-of-Time.
And the dark muscular one,   Below-the-Galleon-Decks.
And the remembered one named,   Palm-Thatch-Floor.
And the little one called,   Fruit-of-the-Distant-Weep
    (mothered black,   from sleeping).

        5

Lady Song-of-Jamestown   mending her fishnets
pulled the water-hook   from my hand.

        6

"Lady Song-of-Jamestown, what shovels you?" I shouted
over my shoulder   and turning
struck her   with my net handle
and broke off the deep brown arm   of   Below-The-
    Galleon-Decks
and drug and drug . . .

        7

When at last I got to farthest other shore
I turned to Fruit-of-the-Distant-Weep   saying,
"O chile   for what you sleeping?   Look
at the ripe groceries on the overhanging branch,"   and
    grabbing
my gray-spined spear   reached up
to tap a bag in the cluster of bags
into the canoe   and with my blade,   halfed it:
toast   mollusky iron telescope pipes   and the posted reward.

8

And though silence descended on Tapping-Out-of-Time
and Palm-Thatch-Floor reeled in some distance,
the Wept-Slept chile   flew open and smiled
scooped up fondles of sea moss   and threw at my feet.

9

And inching along the gunwales
I danced   and danced   "The pushed walk."

FLAGELLIFORM 7

There been a long-term betrayal. You could tell
by a certain fitchy smell. A brotha could tell.
Somehow by hook or by boat or by footwork
or by the trail of leaking beta particles
there been a spectacular spit-shiningly precise
decay. Who/when was one question, and one
question was protected by a layer of asbestos,
a decagon fence, a constant squall of laws—
law of Signs, law of Co-signs, third law of
Thumbtacks, law of the Jungle Bunny,
and the long-neglected Black Code and centering
it all, the impossibility of Absolute Zero, bro.
Still, it cold. It made a brotha want to be sure
to get his words' worth, his ass blackened ass
movin'. Soon it be night and then the equational
epitaphs be dictated and then it be like a crime
scene, the masses of botfly larvae wiggling
the surface of the epidermis, and a faint scent
of fission. Who knew then what the mission
would be knew the weaponry of his so-called
clan and best be ready to wash hisself in the ritual
dried leaf bath and resist. The impulse to gag
or the impulse to group, impurity as information,
information as leash or history or a dollop
of dream dispensed by a pair of lazy tongs,
that much hisself knew. Fucks hisself grandly

with a pair of lazy tongs, he do-dee-do-dee-do.
In the middle, the cleft, where it don't matter.
He riding that swishy fissure like a wish-you-
were-here. He a bad muther—shut-yo-mouth.
He licked it once. He liked it. He trying hard to—

FLAGELLIFORM 21: EXILE ("TO BE
SURE, HOT WATER KILLS A MAN, BUT
COLD WATER TOO KILLS A MAN.")

Mama said for safety we wander.

I remember different lands.

One where soldiers showed me
where all's future war,
war signs tow and end,
shined higher. That's the word: knack.
In the lands we traveled
they give me 'war knack,'
a dunk leer to target the target,
an inner spring sword motor.

One land I learned to track without phone.
Put a notch in a lion.
I learned *serum full a fool that's larger*:
how to wield bladed
phrases, bang
the proverb stick.

Higher abhorred words weirdly near inured
me from getting bashed, an "um"
so dense shimmer designed
could brain the louchest tête.

Another place the General show me
wires for leering, den rug nerve potions,
ant-ish valance spy gels, making the phones
workin the inner spring and sway.

And once I learned . . .   woe   the whir
   groom white skinned lion.

                                 : Tell me about it, Trawler.

All this before they came   to call me

Bone Breaking Lion   Son of the Buffalo   Cats
   on the Shoulder

I   just a kid.

I'm in the big stick and the big stick is in me. The walls are
porous with mold and inactivity. The black-and-tans are foamy
round the rim and cool and rich and short-haired and well-
trained and on patrol. Flammable hydrocarbon. It is the fourth
month in the French revolutionary calendar, always. No one
knows what happened to the fifth. Flammable hydrocarbon
jelly. I knew once but my hack became a habit and I coughed. In
here they teach us how to move our hips, some dance called the
Black Bottom and some dance called the Gimp. We like it. I am
unsure if there is another bivalve in the joint. Just plain happy
to have the help. Flammable hydrocarbon jelly as condiment.
Funnily enough my rusted stenography has finally come in
handy. Oooh, oooh the walls are ever so rounding. See? Dear
big stick on me like a hurt. Sometimes I forget about adjusting
my I-beam thinking cap and I have to move out and bivouac it
in the open gummy terrain. There are seeds and roving packs
of clouds—I stay out of their way and they leave me alone.
Flammable hydrocarbon jelly as condiment as confinement.
According to the knobs in the wall it is somewhere between
Dec. 21 and Jan. 19. I don't know which way South is, which
is in a way a relief. Pleased to report haven't been picking at
what am still convinced is an intimate case of keratosis. O'
Icecap, I am icebound and there is a clunk somewhere in my
lazier eye. I glanced away from my firing pin for one wobbly
second (one!) and it kerplunked. Gone. Nada. Finito. How ya
like me now. The cylindrical nature of days here does that to a

body. I long for my firing pin, my fireside chats and a glass. Any type of glass will do, for any type of two-way chew. Flammable hydrocarbon jelly as condiment as confinement as document. Weird to be so intimate with the weather.

FLAGELLIFORM 3

If it itchy if the falling
rhythm if the clanking of his
clamp if the hatchet glinting
in the swingy lamplight
if the beta particles hit
the illuminating screen betraying
the long crimson lie if it sticky
if possibly maybe perhaps the
tightness if his asking for it if the
ancestors say *move your feet when
you pray* if the havoc of arrival
threatened to rip a seam in
time if *I'm a hustler baby,
I just want you to know* if no one
could tell him what procedure
going to be done if the high road
wasps dangerously if bitch don't
need to if the war babies war
behind their chunky grates if the brassy
fields is glassy with mandibles if he
clammy in his hand if his ascetic
weaponry made it tricky if the diagrams
in the handbook for identification
of poisonous if he gassed
the looking glass if the sense of if if if
corpuscles is muscular in their wafty

way if the sentence of a nervous
period is a straight line if period if he
soda soda soda so-dah so-duh
soooo-daaaa so if *put your damn*
hands up, y'all got to feel me
if *Akpeteshie* is for libation firstly
if weak footwork made it simpler
to trap the if the if
                        he clap
if the passkey was rendered
in putty if the strap further
cinched if *all my true dog niggers,*
put your damn hands up
if sambo sambo sambo sam-bone
some-buh sam-boy samba salvo
salve salvationist sanctuary sand-blind
fuck y'all salute saaaaah-mmmm-bow
and arrow if warty tar makes for
good smoked if bone in yuh
nose if the self-tunnelling worm
drive if he not tellin' if he hidin' up
in the thermals if *I just wanna love ya,*
and be who I am if the thermals is
habitual if they patted him
down if the thatchy that-away
sign concealed the if the gauzy
pistol an equation if
if & was—

FLAGELLIFORM 45

Incoming!

> With the two-edged
> they hit me twister

> (Wind or the wounded air)

Then they twinkled there

> as a fresh rivulet

 on the starchy road

> as now I lay me
> down beside my innards

 How like them

(Wind or the wounded air)

> pleating before the screaming
> dive bomber squadron—

This's what I gots fer ya:

> my tattered but lusty umbrella
> hand-lettered with the words: "No I am the
>   mission target"

Awaiting the in-coming   Secret Throbbing
                                                I confess:

an internal parallax   an impure glass   an incessant
                                                    pendulous tick

      confounds me

And them unloaded

And as them leaving them asking: Ever forgotten how to fly?

Stupid sucky   How to fly?
With a goiter necklace of such
heft often I can't even get up

And then   them all goed home

That's the trouble with them   Them always just shy

Often I wish
could they finish
the whole job once-and-for—I so like them smell
                           They yeasty

They keep a back-up distraction of wood
anemones mouthing along to my only hear: *I never could,*
    I never could

Nevertheless
I get it on   good information:

                    A label on each shiny missile
                    reads Year of Grace No.___

There is nothing left too little

The twisted remains

A shredded welcome mat and persistent drizzle

From the rubble the official issue
first-aid kit issuing a self-adhesive yell:

They would, they really really would

FLAGELLIFORM 50

Whosoever woodrats is scurrilous   boldfaces
the I-beam thinking cap

I been a knuckler

Hiss: hour hand irrigating with impurities
my vigilant headgear

            (seeding) meadow grasses

                    (seeding) mea culpas

stooping the rafters
      of the hereafter
      to wastepaper

Hairy wonders
unyoked and filling with gradual
snowblinding speed—

Fear of the wicks. Fear of the sacred creamy air.
Fear of the debriefings on precisely which sweet
know-nothings were blown into him. Which
is a question he swells within. Which, he holds
the dark lantern to, and thus. Thus reveals
the sung-dread of the receding trail. Dread
of the breach of the sign warning of snowberries.
Dread of the sliding place. Awe of the night
disease. Awe of the waste-part remaining.
Awe of the dog child's heavings. A dog child's
stitching gait. His dark red hog, his brindled
hog tongue. An earless dog of the earless ones.
A dog an offering for the hammer mechanism.
Palatable is the sacrifice for the pitted tusk.
Pitiful in the redness without cover. Pitiful
in his muskgarment. "I go naked on the way
to Bolga." Where the adobe weapons end
in septums. From the hooks and the searing.
From the splaying and the quiet. The tunneling
wind through his wet cage. Younger brother
of the earless ones, those Afrogothic. Out
from a giant growth come a noise. Out from
a pustular growth come a hanging. Out from
a jaundiced growth come the tail swinging its
length. Out from a pulsing growth come

the ash-smudged necks. Born in the time
when clay pots dotted his carrion farms.
"I bind the glowing worm in the forehead."

FLAGELLIFORM 19: "SNAKE FOOT
THAT DOES NOT WALK."

Gathered my owls. My falcons. My archers. My horses
and their men. My friends and my axes.
My guns, my near north spears. My arrows.
My tents and my battle chants. My dogs.

At Tabon, near Kita city.   At Gettysburg.   At Tikrit.
At Lake Erie   At the Bastille   At the Nile
At Vimy   At Ypres   At Santa Clara
At Moncada   At Las Mercedes
    At Tambov
At Petrograd   At *La Semaine Sanglante*
At the Communards' Wall in the Père Lachaise Cemetery
In the rue Ramponeau in Belleville.

We were fewer   We were fever

At Fallujah.   At Khe Sanh   At Vicksburg
    At Lake Champlain
At My Lai.   At the Sunni Triangle

We   lay   "All our wonders
                              unavenged"

FLAGELLIFORM 39: AND THE NAME
OF THAT SPEAR WAS, ONE PLACE
WHERE IT ENTERS, NINE PLACES
WHERE THE BLOOD COMES OUT

I see him. I have him.
He sits on his black-coated horse.
Towards leaches,
swamp fingers dank
in ragged beef smells.
In spike-horned hat. Natural, open.
The very war fin suit cage.
Uber welded.

We are a rigid door thin space apart.
Close enough to smell his blue saddle vapor
his musick

flame-quick   reappearing him

on a far away
                    red ridge

a go-word   burned   into us.

FLAGELLIFORM 79

And out of clammy havoc

                at the Egypt of intention

Preparing the instruments
Pressurizing the cramp

I missed them so

And the pick pick pick pick   choke   pick choke   pick
Of the yellowed roily ministrant machinery—

Ol' Trawler's a sport

Ol' Trawler staring into his passbook
all through the scrubbing the shaving down

                the ancient hacksaw shaded
                by a blind corner
                wasping quietly away

(I love my away)

And in the grand
old tradition   an oath
of asbestosis demanded of all official witnesses

                    (I love my witnesses)

        And finger painted fingers on a Pharaonic
        platter pointing the proof

I close mine eyes
(I love my proof)
I creating a little lesson

Do I swear?

I cradling a little lesion

Who you talkin' to Ol' Trawler?

Easy now partner just lie back and mouth along:

>O' but there's a certain thawed realm
>curtained by a fence of lovely thermals
>where   we'll ride   we'll ride   we'll ride
>the Cyclobenzaprine stitch
>till there's nothing more
>and I am dumb on the stop bath floor

Is easy now right? Is funky now—Keep it funky
Is where at last the digging starts
when I go down at last
drowsy from a heady brewed
ready-mix of Morning Stars
embedded in my I-beam thinking cap

Day is done   Shut up   *Gone the sun*

The spades is digging in
and I can't do nuffin'

They here   They *in*
They botching in no matter
what   They really
                         Gone the earth

A suite of fine aways   A malpractice of sleeps

Going the little mine sky—

"World Town." The title comes from a song title off M.I.A.'s album *Kala*.

"Security of the First World." The title comes from a song title off Public Enemy's album *It Takes a Nation of Millions to Hold Us Back*.

"Mack Daddy Manifesto." The epigraph comes from *The Communist Manifesto* by Karl Marx and Friedrich Engels. The poem includes lines sampled from *The Communist Manifesto* and Sigmund Freud's *The Ego and the Id*.

"The Collected Novellas of Gilbert Ryle." The novella titles and some of the novellas themselves are built from language and ideas in Gilbert Ryle's *The Concept of Mind*.

"A Laborious Wakefulness or Was It a Most Unapologetic Whistling in the Ear." The title and some of the language (italicized and otherwise) comes out of and thinks into Descartes' *Meditations I and II*.

"Chinese Blow Up Doll" is for Gil Scott-Heron. The poem samples phrases from his poem "Evolution (And Flashback)" off his album *Small Talk at 125th and Lenox* and his poem "Ain't No New Thing" off his album *Free Will*.

"H.N.I.C." includes lines sampled from Laura Locoul Gore's *Memories of the Old Plantation Home* and the Federal Writers' Project collection *Slave Narratives: A Folk History of Slavery in the U.S. from Interviews with Former Slaves.*

The West African epic of Sundiata inspired the thinking and action in some of the Flagelliforms.

"Flagelliform 21: Exile ('To be sure, hot water kills a man, But cold water too kills a man.')." The parenthetical portion of the subtitle is a quotation from the Sundiata epic. "Bone Breaking Lion," "Son of the Buffalo," and "Cats on the Shoulder" are Sundiata's praise names.

"Flagelliform 3" samples lyrics from Jay-Z's "I Just Wanna Love You (Give It 2 Me)" off his album *The Dynasty: Roc La Familia* and "Izzo (H.O.V.A.)" off his album *The Blueprint.*

"Flagelliform 19: 'Snake Foot That Does Not Walk.'" The subtitle is a quotation from the Sundiata epic. The quoted phrase in the final line is the title of a book by Don Domanski.

"Flagelliform 39: And the Name of That Spear Was, One Place Where It Enters, Nine Places Where the Blood Comes Out." The subtitle is a quotation from the Sundiata epic. The spear belongs to Sundiata.